Little Riddlers

Staffordshire

Edited By Jenni Harrison

First published in Great Britain in 2018 by:

YoungWriters

Young Writers
Remus House
Coltsfoot Drive
Peterborough
PE2 9BF
Telephone: 01733 890066
Website: www.youngwriters.co.uk

All Rights Reserved
Book Design by Ashley Janson
© Copyright Contributors 2018
SB ISBN 978-1-78896-486-9
Printed and bound in the UK by BookPrintingUK
Website: www.bookprintinguk.com
YB0362W

FOREWORD

Dear Reader,

Are you ready to get your thinking caps on to puzzle your way through this wonderful collection?

Young Writers' Little Riddlers competition set out to encourage young writers to create their own riddles. Their answers could be whatever or whoever their imaginations desired; from people to places, animals to objects, food to seasons. Riddles are a great way to further the children's use of poetic expression, including onomatopoeia and similes, as well as encourage them to 'think outside the box' by providing clues without giving the answer away immediately.

All of us here at Young Writers believe in the importance of inspiring young children to produce creative writing, including poetry, and we feel that seeing their own riddles in print will keep that creative spirit burning brightly and proudly.

We hope you enjoy riddling your way through this book as much as we enjoyed reading all the entries.

CONTENTS

Birchwood Primary School, Dordon

Daniel Potts (7)	1
Bella Nicole Alison Osborne (7)	2
Daniel Ward (6)	3
Jensen Winter (6)	4
Mitchell Haywood (7)	5
Alexander Haywood (7)	6
Alexia Bailey-Johnson (6)	7
Charlotte Eley (7)	8
Zane Andrew Everitt (6)	9
Amelia Blower (7)	10
Sophie Spencer (7)	11
Alfie Hopkins (7)	12
Amy Jools Thomas (7)	13
Amelia Palfrey (7)	14
Korlie Healey (6)	15
Joshua Robinson (7)	16
Chloe Louise French (6)	17
Sophie Isabella Smith (7)	18
Emile Bubinaite (6)	19
Jack Cope (7)	20
Holly Brown (7)	21
Aimee-Louise Hall (7)	22
Lillie-May Chatwin (6)	23
Charlie Taylor (7)	24
Max Taylor (6)	25
Leighton Craig Cowley-Evans (7)	26
Jessica Read (7)	27
Taylor Brown (7)	28
Cassey Buchanan (6)	29
Erin Harrison (6)	30
Amélie Goldsmith (6)	31
Jimmy-Dean Paul Smith (6)	32
James Stevenson (7)	33
Mya Brook (5)	34
George Barlow (6)	35
Kai Sheppard (7)	36
Braydan Webb (6)	37
Hadley Faultless (7)	38
Louie Ogilvie (7)	39
William Franks (7)	40
Henry Cooper (5)	41
Romee-Lea Mendez (5)	42
Mason Spragg-Hateley (6)	43
Bobby Hankinson (6)	44
Georgie Gilbert (5)	45
Martyna Goldas (5)	46
Faye Lily Petford (6)	47
Paige Olivia Webb (5)	48
Evie Harrison (6)	49
Alfie Hassall (6)	50
Olivia Grace Reading (7)	51
Sammy Barber (7)	52
Daisy Smith (5)	53
Evan Cart (5)	54
Zachary Osborne (6)	55
Jude Edwards (5)	56
Jacob Chatwin (5)	57
Kaleb Baily Ferris (5)	58
Troy Todd-Dolphin (6)	59
Zac Turner (7)	60
Mia Hopper (6)	61
Riley Johnstone (6)	62
Elsie-May Spears (6)	63
Alfie James Lamb (6)	64
Alfie Bartlam (5)	65
Kyle Ross (6)	66
Nithil Diyon Obberiyage Fonseka (6)	67
Tommy Spragg (6)	68

Elsie Mellor (6)	69
Lailah Harper (5)	70
Hester Dark (5)	71
Rory White (5)	72
Cassidy Bradford (5)	73
Ollie O'Carroll (5)	74
Tyler Flint (6)	75
Sophia Finch (5)	76
Isobelle Wootton (6)	77
Ethan Allen (6)	78
Lacey Mason (5)	79
Ellie Celella (6)	80
Zac Read (5)	81
Lola Haywood (5)	82
Stanley Cornelius (5)	83
Harry Smitten (5)	84
Millie Broderick (5)	85
Finlay Hart (5)	86
Pal Vyas (5)	87
Sophie Irving (5)	88
Riley James Bullivant-Hughes (5)	89
Tayla Jane McHugh (5)	90

Langdale Primary School, Clayton

Samuel Butters (7)	91
Poppy Turner (7)	92
George Owen (7)	93
Evie Violet Elizabeth Capewell (7)	94
Orla Hindhaugh (6)	95
Edward Pointon (7)	96
Ava Nadin (7)	97
Kian Morgan (6)	98
Vivienne Burke (6)	99
Charlotte Brunt (7)	100
Franklin Garvey (7)	101
Charlotte Lello (7)	102
Hudhaifa AlGhannam (7)	103

Moorgate Primary Academy, Moorgate

Florence Smith (7)	104
Myla McKay-Hunter (5)	105
Jasmine Krumina (6)	106
Blake Antony McNeill (6)	107
Bethany Hunt (5)	108
Corey Dempster (6)	109
Le-Ha Dao (7)	110
Jayden Ollie Ryley (5)	111
Maja Joanna Rynkun (5)	112
Molly Olivia Seal (7)	113
Daisy Kathleen Brookes (7)	114
James Ian John Thompson (7)	115
Peyton Mills-Deakin (5)	116
Lacey-Rae Reynolds (6)	117
Seb Hunt (6)	118
Shayla Ann Crowley (6)	119
Jayden Marsh (6)	120
Mason Yeo Powles (7)	121
Oscar Friend (5)	122
Maggie Pemperton (6)	123
Ethan Andrew Bennett (7)	124
Alfie Patrick Butler (5)	125
Erin Rose James (6)	126
Arnav Singh (6)	127
Bethany-Rose Silver (6)	128
Dante McGrath (7)	129
Albie George Hollis (5)	130
Luca Bishop (5)	131
Emanuela Ayline Bogdan (6)	132
Lucy Hughes (6)	133
Alina Mihaela Lungu (7)	134
Jayden Jennings (6)	135
Lola Holly Brennan (5)	136
Henry Hinkley (6)	137
Oscar Harvey Duerden (6)	138
Lilly Bonkowska (5)	139
Christian-Denis Ionita (5)	140
Isla Louise De,aubeney James (5)	141
Emilia Jurkiewicz (6)	142

St Augustine's RC (A) Primary School, Meir

Melody Sentulio (6)	143
Alphonsina Nsimi (6)	144
George Ikins (5)	145
Lydia Freyah Minister (6)	146
Oliver Grajcar (6)	147
Hibbah Amin (5)	148
Jenson Bayley Ayres (6)	149
Tiffany Maziwisa (6)	150
Indie Anna Mary Reynolds (6)	151
Tayden Arif Gratton (5)	152

St John's CE (A) Primary School, Trent Vale

Arahbela Arvesu (6)	153

St Peter's CE First School, Marchington

Scarlett Pearson (5)	154
Joseph Orme (6)	155
William Stanley Goodwin (6)	156
Mason Joseph (7)	157
Lily Rose Hawkins (6)	158
Evelyn Ball (6)	159
Barney Ward (6)	160
Matthew Neale (6)	161
Ellie Louise Buxton (7)	162
Edan Hall (6)	163
Sienna-Rose Horton (6)	164
William Hayhurst (6)	165
Korey Gildart (5)	166

THE POEMS

Little Riddlers 2018 - Staffordshire

What Am I?

My favourite food is new green leaves on the trees
I am as big as a rhino
I have feet like a door and big ears
My habitat is the African plains
I like playing in the day
I have old grey skin
I can swim, but don't be fooled, I'm not a fish
I sleep under the night sky
My head is very big and wrinkly
I am grey and dull
I love rolling in a patch of dark brown mud
I am old and dull.
What am I?

Answer: An elephant.

Daniel Potts (7)
Birchwood Primary School, Dordon

What Am I?

I live in grassland and below ground
You can keep me as a pet but I might bite you
I have fluffy, silky fur and I'm cuddly
My nose is as black as midnight
All of my family have one tooth that's super white
I do not like birds because they fly after me
I have two stubby, short legs
I have big floppy ears
I eat carrots and grass
I have a cotton wool tail as white as snow.
What am I?

Answer: A rabbit.

Bella Nicole Alison Osborne (7)
Birchwood Primary School, Dordon

What Am I?

I can destroy a small ship in one bite
The bite is strong enough to kill
My upper body is grey and my lower body is white
Watch out for my sharp teeth
I am the terror of the sea
My home is the sea
You might see me if my fin is out of the water
I may bite divers
I stay under a hundred metres
I weigh a thousand kilograms.
What am I?

Answer: A great white shark.

Daniel Ward (6)
Birchwood Primary School, Dordon

Fierce And Scary

I live in the deep blue sea and snap ships in half
I swipe pirates off their ship
I am a monster and fierce
I have rows and rows of sharp teeth and I eat pirates
I have razor-sharp teeth that gobble up pirates
I don't leave anything when I gobble them up
I have tentacles that can stick to anything, they're like glowing glue.
Who am I?

Answer: The kraken.

Jensen Winter (6)
Birchwood Primary School, Dordon

King Of The Jungle

My brilliant, fantastic, famous brother is Godzilla
He's one of me
I eat really nice bananas
I swing from tree to tree like a flash
I am the strongest animal you have ever seen
I steal food, I'm a cheeky animal
I thump my belly and I jump
I can live in a zoo
I fight other animals
I love to hug.
What am I?

Answer: A gorilla.

Mitchell Haywood (7)
Birchwood Primary School, Dordon

Fluffy And Bouncy

Hello there, I am small like a lunch box
I live in a metal cage
I have two legs to jump on
I am fluffy like a girl's hair
I have eyes like a human
I drink water out of a cup
I have big bushy ears that cuddle my face
I eat bright orange carrots
I am the most cuddly creature
I always like a carrot to munch on.
What am I?

Answer: A rabbit.

Alexander Haywood (7)
Birchwood Primary School, Dordon

Bounce, Bounce

I am so fluffy
I have a twitching nose
I have sharp nails and teeth
I love to eat crunchy carrots
I love to jump up and down
My paws are cute and pink
I have a circle tail that does not move
I love to hop and play
People love to stroke me and pet me
I can be a pet and live in a bunny hole.
What am I?

Answer: A fluffy bunny.

Alexia Bailey-Johnson (6)
Birchwood Primary School, Dordon

What Am I?

I am soft, cute and cuddly and fun to play with
I can have long or short hair and for fun you can comb it
I have four little legs and a fluffy tail like a rabbit and cotton wool
Be warned, I can accidentally hurt you with my nails and teeth
I eat juicy carrots and dandelions
I love to go fast, fast, fast.
What am I?

Answer: A guinea pig.

Charlotte Eley (7)
Birchwood Primary School, Dordon

What Am I?

I have white eyes
When you see me, you will be terrified
My roar can wake up the kraken
I am a gigantic animal
No one will have me as a pet
I will bite them with my sharp teeth
My teeth are like razors
Everyone will scream at me and run around
I have a tail
My tail is like a sword.
What am I?

Answer: A dinosaur.

Zane Andrew Everitt (6)
Birchwood Primary School, Dordon

The Beauty

I live in the warmest barn
You can plait my hair
I like to eat golden hay
My favourite food is carrots
You can ride on my wobbly back
I am kind but sometimes grumpy
Anything can be my enemy, even a human
If you didn't know, there can be lots of me
You have to feed me every day.
What am I?

Answer: A horse.

Amelia Blower (7)
Birchwood Primary School, Dordon

Little Riddlers 2018 - Staffordshire

Fluffy And White

I live in a towering tree, in a hole in the centre of the tree
My eyes glow in the dark night sky
I also fly in the deep dark night
You can only see me at night
I am so fluffy like a teddy bear
I have big wings so I can fly fast
I have lots of feathers
I have a big fluffy, fluffy head.
What am I?

Answer: An owl.

Sophie Spencer (7)
Birchwood Primary School, Dordon

I Am Spiky

If these terrifying humans try to shoot me or go close to me
I will raise my razor-sharp points on the side of me.
If you scare me, I will chase you and it will be really painful and you won't like it.
I live in the depths of the sea
If you try to find me, I can blow up into a big ball.
What am I?

Answer: A pufferfish.

Alfie Hopkins (7)
Birchwood Primary School, Dordon

Squeak!

I am a tiny, furry creature who loves fresh cheese
Cats chase me very often
I squeak and I have whiskers
I am grey, I live in a house
I have tiny razor-sharp teeth
I have four little feet and legs
I don't like cats
I have four pink feet
My nails are as sharp as a knife.
What am I?

Answer: A mouse.

Amy Jools Thomas (7)
Birchwood Primary School, Dordon

Fluffy Bouncer

I can live in a house
I can flap my ears
I can be different colours only if you spot me
I like to eat carrots
I am very, very furry
You can just squeeze me
I think you will love me
I also have big squishy paws
I have sharp white teeth at the front of my mouth.
What am I?

Answer: A bunny.

Amelia Palfrey (7)
Birchwood Primary School, Dordon

Little Riddlers 2018 - Staffordshire

Fly From A Tree

I am nocturnal
I like to fly down
I live in a forest, my home is in a tree
I can have yellow eyes, but I don't
That's a different type of me
I can be a trusted pet, but I have to be in a cage
I can't be eaten
I make this noise... *tu-whit tu-whoo.*
What am I?

Answer: An owl.

Korlie Healey (6)
Birchwood Primary School, Dordon

What Am I?

I have big black spots
I also have short white fur
My nose is as black as can be
My flapping ears can be annoying
My number one enemies are cats, I hate cats
People think I'm the cutest thing on Earth, and I am
People think I'm so cute, they say I'm adorable.
What am I?

Answer: A Dalmatian.

Joshua Robinson (7)
Birchwood Primary School, Dordon

What Am I?

I am cute and fluffy
I hate dogs but I like cats
I like to drink milk
I normally hear dogs bark
I don't like thunder at all
I can be a nocturnal animal
I'm cute and fluffy
I eat mice and rats
I kill mice and rats for my dinner
I have toys that are fun.
What am I?

Answer: A cat.

Chloe Louise French (6)
Birchwood Primary School, Dordon

What's My Name?

My favourite thing to do is swim, especially on a hot and sunny day in the Caribbean
I feast on delicious, scaly and juicy fish
I lurk in the shadows of Davy Jones' locker
You don't want to see my blood-covered teeth
I am the bravest king of the sea you will ever see.
What am I?

Answer: A shark.

Sophie Isabella Smith (7)
Birchwood Primary School, Dordon

Furry Pet

I have furry ears, furry fur
Often people like to stroke me.
If you look closely, you will see brown on my fur
I have a soaking wet nose
I have a person who takes care of me because I am a pet
Watch out, because I hate cats
If you are friendly, I will like you.
What am I?

Answer: A dog.

Emile Bubinaite (6)
Birchwood Primary School, Dordon

What Am I?

I am a fast, brave animal
I'm covered in dark spots
I run as fast as a blue wave
I live in the deep dark forest
My fur is as golden as the sun
I eat any meat
I'm as yellow as paint
My favourite food is deer
My teeth are as sharp as razors.
What am I?

Answer: A cheetah.

Jack Cope (7)
Birchwood Primary School, Dordon

The Mysterious Howler

I prowl around my gloomy, dark cave
It's as dark as coal
In the pitch-black sky at night, I sit on the cliff side
Howling like a clap of thunder
You would be terrified to have me as a loyal pet
Normally I come in the colours black, white, brown and grey.
What am I?

Answer: A wolf.

Holly Brown (7)
Birchwood Primary School, Dordon

Fluffy And Cuddly

I have long thin whiskers
I can be kept as a trusted pet
I have a wagging tail
I am fluffy and cuddly and I walk on four paws
I can come in all different shapes and sizes
I have sharp teeth so I can chew meat
You can see me mostly in the park or on my walk.
What am I?

Answer: A dog.

Aimee-Louise Hall (7)
Birchwood Primary School, Dordon

Slow Creature

I am very slow and green
I have a dark green shell with patterns on it
I hide away from seagulls
I love the deep blue sea
I have some babies
I have a hole in my shell
I have four feet and three toes on every foot
My legs are very short.
What am I?

Answer: A turtle.

Lillie-May Chatwin (6)
Birchwood Primary School, Dordon

The Mean Guy

I'm black so I camouflage at night
I have razor-sharp white, yucky teeth
You can see me in a jungle because it is my habitat
I have sparkly, red, beady eyes
I'm one of the most dangerous creatures in the world
I have a pink tongue.
What am I?

Answer: A panther.

Charlie Taylor (7)
Birchwood Primary School, Dordon

Creature In The Depths

I lurk in the depths of the waters
You never know when I'm under you
I like to feast on pirates
My eyes are as green as emeralds
My tentacles can cut a ship in half
I have rows and rows of sharp teeth
My suckers are as sticky as glue.
Who am I?

Answer: The kraken.

Max Taylor (6)
Birchwood Primary School, Dordon

Little Beast

I have eight skinny legs
I am as fast as a cat
I live in small holes and houses
I jump out and scare people day and night
I creep outside in summer
I can climb upside down
I have a little head
You may find me outside or inside.
What am I?

Answer: A spider.

Leighton Craig Cowley-Evans (7)
Birchwood Primary School, Dordon

Lovely Pet

Some days I chase cats, because I don't like them at all
I like the way I come in different shapes and sizes
I like how I start small and grow bigger
My owner makes me stay in a cage
Lots of people get me from the pet shop.
What am I?

Answer: A dog.

Jessica Read (7)
Birchwood Primary School, Dordon

The Fierce Beast

I may look cute but I am fierce
I have black and orange fur
My fur can protect me from other animals
My four legs are for walking on
My ears are for hearing
My tail is black like the night sky and orange like a carrot.
What am I?

Answer: A tiger.

Taylor Brown (7)
Birchwood Primary School, Dordon

A Snow Lover

You can't keep me as a pet because I will eat you up
You can spot me in the snowy, towering mountains
I like to hunt warm-blooded prey
You may think I am a fast cheetah but I'm not
I am white and I love snow.
What am I?

Answer: A snow leopard.

Cassey Buchanan (6)
Birchwood Primary School, Dordon

Fierce Beast

You won't see me unless you have brilliant eyesight
My favourite food is zebra or gazelle
I like to pounce on my prey
I live in the savannah
I lurk in the shadows in the grass
My ears are very sensitive.
What am I?

Answer: A lion.

Erin Harrison (6)
Birchwood Primary School, Dordon

What Am I?

I have big, long ears
Did you know that I eat healthy carrots?
When I wake up, I hop outside
Then I play with my friends Chloe, Eve, Olivia and Cassy in the day
I have big green eyes
My friends like me.
What am I?

Answer: A bunny.

Amélie Goldsmith (6)
Birchwood Primary School, Dordon

What Am I?

I can't swim in the deep blue water
I am red as a heart
I am as soft as a polar bear
You can keep me as a pet
I live in a cage and run very quickly on a wheel
I like walking on soft stuff.
What am I?

Answer: A hamster.

Jimmy-Dean Paul Smith (6)
Birchwood Primary School, Dordon

The Scary Slithery Creature

I love to slither
I have green scales
I might bite you when I'm angry, so be careful
I leave a trail when I slither
I don't have a shell
I usually have long teeth and red eyes to hunt prey.
What am I?

Answer: A snake.

James Stevenson (7)
Birchwood Primary School, Dordon

What Am I?

I have a long grey tail
My skin is silvery grey
I have four big legs
I have hair sticking up on my forehead
I have a super-duper curly trunk
I have a little grey circle at the bottom of my tail.
What am I?

Answer: An elephant.

Mya Brook (5)
Birchwood Primary School, Dordon

What Am I?

My favourite food to feast on is juicy fish
My favourite hobby is jumping on the rocks
My most feared enemies are seals
Every time I dive in the fish hide
My wings help me swim
I'm in danger.
What am I?

Answer: A penguin.

George Barlow (6)
Birchwood Primary School, Dordon

A Slithering Beast

I have a long tail and teeth as sharp as knives
I slither with a quiet sound
I am very big and long
You will see my scales if you look
You will hear me if you hear a quiet, scary hissing sound.
What am I?

Answer: A python.

Kai Sheppard (7)
Birchwood Primary School, Dordon

What Am I?

My food is sixty mice every week
In my tank, I curl up into a ball in my lovely home
I have stripes all over me
My name is Steve, I slither
My tail smacks on the wall.
What am I?

Answer: A snake.

Braydan Webb (6)
Birchwood Primary School, Dordon

A Feathered Creature

I have wings and fly in the freezing air
I like to stretch my beautiful, magnificent wings and flap about
I have a yellow beak
I have red and blue feathers all over my body.
What am I?

Answer: A parrot.

Hadley Faultless (7)
Birchwood Primary School, Dordon

What Am I?

I sunbathe all day
I speedily run after my prey
I am a vicious flesh eater
I love to eat juicy red meat
My fur is as golden as the sun
I'm king of all beasts.
What am I?

Answer: A lion.

Louie Ogilvie (7)
Birchwood Primary School, Dordon

What Am I?

I like to eat slimy, slippery fish
I live in the Amazon
I like to live in murky water
I'm scared of salmon
I might kill people
I love to swim in caves.
What am I?

Answer: A catfish.

William Franks (7)
Birchwood Primary School, Dordon

Speedy

I am the fastest in Africa
I have black spots
I have four yellow and black legs
I can stalk people
I can climb up trees
I am furry
I eat meat.
What am I?

Answer: A cheetah.

Henry Cooper (5)
Birchwood Primary School, Dordon

Slimy

I am patterned
I am slimy
I have a red tongue
I make a hissing sound
I have no legs
I have beady eyes
I am scaly
I live in the jungle.
What am I?

Answer: A snake.

Romee-Lea Mendez (5)
Birchwood Primary School, Dordon

What Am I?

I eat people when they come close to me
I roar when people are near
I kill people who come close to me
I live in the woods
I have very long claws.
What am I?

Answer: A lion.

Mason Spragg-Hateley (6)
Birchwood Primary School, Dordon

What Am I?

I have a lovely, long, curly tail
I have four little legs
I make a weird noise
I am a bit little
I am very pink
I begin with a 'P'.
What am I?

Answer: A pig.

Bobby Hankinson (6)
Birchwood Primary School, Dordon

Sharp Claws

I have sharp claws
I am cute
I move slowly when I creep on a mouse
I live in a house
I move quickly when I smell food
I go *miaow*.
What am I?

Answer: A cat.

Georgie Gilbert (5)
Birchwood Primary School, Dordon

What Am I?

I have a curly tail
I have a pink coat
I live on a farm
I love rolling in the mud
I am smelly
I have green eyes
I have four legs.
What am I?

Answer: A pig.

Martyna Goldas (5)
Birchwood Primary School, Dordon

Rudolph

I have long ears
I live in the forest
My favourite food is moss
I have grey fur
I grow antlers every summer
I have hooves.
What am I?

Answer: A reindeer.

Faye Lily Petford (6)
Birchwood Primary School, Dordon

Grey

I have a long trunk
I am grey
I live in India or Africa
I drink water out of my nose
I have a long tail
I have four legs.
What am I?

Answer: An elephant.

Paige Olivia Webb (5)
Birchwood Primary School, Dordon

What Am I?

People enjoy riding on my back
I have shoes that need to be changed, how annoying that is
I love carrots because they are juicy.
Do you know what I am?

Answer: A horse.

Evie Harrison (6)
Birchwood Primary School, Dordon

An Antarctic Creature

I am black and white
And you can touch me because I'm safe
I love to swim
I have a bright yellow beak
I have a small beak.
What am I?

Answer: A penguin.

Alfie Hassall (6)
Birchwood Primary School, Dordon

My Cute Pet

I am cute and fluffy
My claws are as sharp as a knife
A wheel is my playground
I live in a cage
You should beware, I can bite.
What am I?

Answer: A hamster.

Olivia Grace Reading (7)
Birchwood Primary School, Dordon

What Am I?

I have black and white fur
I live in the South Pole
I'm a carnivore
I hunt fish
I am not a pet
I have a yellow beak.
What am I?

Answer: A penguin.

Sammy Barber (7)
Birchwood Primary School, Dordon

Fluffy

I have a fluffy body
I have a fluffy mane
I have a fluffy tail
I have a horn
I go *neigh*
I eat leaves and grass.
What am I?

Answer: A unicorn.

Daisy Smith (5)
Birchwood Primary School, Dordon

What Am I?

I live on a farm
I am really smelly
I have a golden ring on my nose
I am a herbivore
I have no fur
I don't have a mane.
What am I?

Answer: A pig.

Evan Cart (5)
Birchwood Primary School, Dordon

What Am I?

Cats are petrified of me
They run away fast
I rip my toys apart like dinner
Chewing things is my favourite
Long walks are fun.
What am I?

Answer: A dog.

Zachary Osborne (6)
Birchwood Primary School, Dordon

Fierce

I have got black spots on my body
I have fierce eyes
I have sharp claws
I am very fast
I am deadly
I have long legs.
What am I?

Answer: A cheetah.

Jude Edwards (5)
Birchwood Primary School, Dordon

Silly

I eat bananas
I have brown fur
I like to jump up and down
I stand on trees
I have a long tail
I live in the jungle.
What am I?

Answer: A monkey.

Jacob Chatwin (5)
Birchwood Primary School, Dordon

What Am I?

I live in hot Africa
I am a big carnivore
I am really yellow
I am very fluffy
I am very fierce
I eat lots of meat.
What am I?

Answer: A lion.

Kaleb Baily Ferris (5)
Birchwood Primary School, Dordon

Slither

I am venomous
I have zero legs
I live in the savannah
I slither
I have a red forked tongue
I have sharp teeth.
What am I?

Answer: A snake.

Troy Todd-Dolphin (6)
Birchwood Primary School, Dordon

Furry Beast

I can climb trees with the claws on the end of my paws
I have razor-sharp teeth
I can bite and scratch you if you pick me up.
What am I?

Answer: A cat.

Zac Turner (7)
Birchwood Primary School, Dordon

What Am I?

I have spiky hair
I have sharp teeth
I live in Africa
I have a long tail
I have long legs
I have a big body.
What am I?

Answer: A lion.

Mia Hopper (6)
Birchwood Primary School, Dordon

Slither

I slither around
I have sharp teeth
I bite my prey
I am scary
I am venomous
I don't live in Antarctica
What am I?

Answer: A snake.

Riley Johnstone (6)
Birchwood Primary School, Dordon

What Am I?

I live in Africa
I have a long wavy tail
I am a herbivore
I have no fur
I have round ears
I am loud.
What am I?

Answer: An elephant.

Elsie-May Spears (6)
Birchwood Primary School, Dordon

What Am I?

I am grey
I live in Africa
I am a herbivore
I have a long trunk
I have a long tail
I have four legs.
What am I?

Answer: An elephant.

Alfie James Lamb (6)
Birchwood Primary School, Dordon

What Am I?

I have a long trunk
I am grey
I eat leaves
I am very big
I drink water
I make a trumpeting sound.
What am I?

Answer: An elephant.

Alfie Bartlam (5)
Birchwood Primary School, Dordon

What Am I?

You may see me in Asia, fighting
I have sharp teeth and claws
I am very strong
I have black and orange stripes.
What am I?

Answer: A tiger.

Kyle Ross (6)
Birchwood Primary School, Dordon

What Am I?

I roar
I have sharp teeth
I am loud
I am scary
I am hungry
I have a long tail
I have golden fur.
What am I?

Answer: A lion.

Nithil Diyon Obberiyage Fonseka (6)
Birchwood Primary School, Dordon

Slow

I have a long tongue
I am long and thin
I have scales
I have terrifying eyes
I slither around the ground.
What am I?

Answer: A snake.

Tommy Spragg (6)
Birchwood Primary School, Dordon

What Am I?

I live in Africa
I am very loud
I have a long tail
I am a carnivore
I am brave
I have a fluffy mane.
What am I?

Answer: A lion.

Elsie Mellor (6)
Birchwood Primary School, Dordon

What Am I?

I have a spiky mane
I am yellow
I have sharp teeth
I live in Africa
I am fearful
I have little legs.
What am I?

Answer: A lion.

Lailah Harper (5)
Birchwood Primary School, Dordon

Fierce

I am furry
I am hungry
I am yellow and black
I am fierce
I have sharp teeth
I have black stripes.
What am I?

Answer: A tiger.

Hester Dark (5)
Birchwood Primary School, Dordon

What Am I?

I swing long in trees
I have a good grip
I eat berries
I have a stripy face
I come from Africa.
What am I?

Answer: A mandrill.

Rory White (5)
Birchwood Primary School, Dordon

Long Neck

I have a long neck
I eat leaves
I am tall
I have black spots
I have four legs
I am yellow.
What am I?

Answer: A giraffe.

Cassidy Bradford (5)
Birchwood Primary School, Dordon

Cute

I have four legs
I have a horn
I am pink
I am magical
I am fluffy
I am very beautiful.
What am I?

Answer: A unicorn.

Ollie O'Carroll (5)
Birchwood Primary School, Dordon

Teeth

I live in the water
I have sharp teeth
I am fast
I am fierce
I scare people
I have fins.
What am I?

Answer: A shark.

Tyler Flint (6)
Birchwood Primary School, Dordon

What Am I?

I am pink and I have a curly tail
I have four pink legs
I have a snorting nose
I have two wavy ears.
What am I?

Answer: A pig.

Sophia Finch (5)
Birchwood Primary School, Dordon

Fuzzy

I have black eyes
I have a short tail
I am fluffy
I have sharp nails
I am brown or yellow.
What am I?

Answer: A hamster.

Isobelle Wootton (6)
Birchwood Primary School, Dordon

What Am I?

I am grey
I have a long trunk
I have teeth to eat leaves
I drink water
I live in Africa.
What am I?

Answer: An elephant.

Ethan Allen (6)
Birchwood Primary School, Dordon

Fuzzy

I can wag my tail
I can have floppy ears
I am cute
I can bark
I will eat anything.
What am I?

Answer: A dog.

Lacey Mason (5)
Birchwood Primary School, Dordon

Fast

I am spotty
I am furry
I am very fast
I purr
I live in Africa
I have four legs.
What am I?

Answer: A cheetah.

Ellie Celella (6)
Birchwood Primary School, Dordon

Fast

I have stripes
I am sneaky
I hide
I live in the jungle
I pounce
I have claws.
What am I?

Answer: A tiger.

Zac Read (5)
Birchwood Primary School, Dordon

What Am I?

I am pink
I have a short tail
I roll in the mud
I have short feet
I live on a farm.
What am I?

Answer: A pig.

Lola Haywood (5)
Birchwood Primary School, Dordon

Little Riddlers 2018 - Staffordshire

What Am I?

I am smelly
I live on a farm
I love going in the mud
I have a curly tail
I am pink.
What am I?

Answer: A pig.

Stanley Cornelius (5)
Birchwood Primary School, Dordon

What Am I?

I live on a farm
I love milk
I am black and white
I eat grass
I sleep standing up.
What am I?

Answer: A cow.

Harry Smitten (5)
Birchwood Primary School, Dordon

Little Riddlers 2018 - Staffordshire

Squirter

I am huge
I have four legs
I eat leaves
I squirt water
I have a trunk.
What am I?

Answer: An elephant.

Millie Broderick (5)
Birchwood Primary School, Dordon

What Am I?

I have a long trunk
I have a long tail
I like the water
I live in Africa.
What am I?

Answer: An elephant.

Finlay Hart (5)
Birchwood Primary School, Dordon

What Am I?

I live on a farm
I am pink
I oink
I love mud
I am dirty
I am sticky.
What am I?

Answer: A pig.

Pal Vyas (5)
Birchwood Primary School, Dordon

What Am I?

I live on a farm
I am pink
I have a curly tail
I am fat
I am muddy.
What am I?

Answer: A pig.

Sophie Irving (5)
Birchwood Primary School, Dordon

What Am I?

I live on a farm
I am small
I love mud
I am pink
I have a wavy tail.
What am I?

Answer: A pig.

Riley James Bullivant-Hughes (5)
Birchwood Primary School, Dordon

What Am I?

I have a little tail
I am pink
I am smelly
I am fat
I am muddy.
What am I?

Answer: A pig.

Tayla Jane McHugh (5)
Birchwood Primary School, Dordon

What Am I?

I look like a tea cosy and I keep you warm in winter
I am made of wool or leather
I feel cosy and warm
I taste a bit funny
Do you know what I am yet?
I look like a little box
I come in all different shapes and sizes
I can be for the summer or the winter.
What am I?

Answer: A hat.

Samuel Butters (7)
Langdale Primary School, Clayton

Build Me

I come in rectangles and squares.
I come in different colours.
You can build a house with me.
I am plastic.
I sound very crackly when you dig in my box.
Have you guessed me yet?
I have little characters too.
What am I?

Answer: Lego.

Poppy Turner (7)
Langdale Primary School, Clayton

The Best Swinger

I eat bananas
I am brown and peach
Do you know what I am yet?
I hang upside down
I say *oo-oo-ooh*
Have you guessed me yet?
I have long legs
I have long arms
I live in the trees
What am I?

Answer: A monkey.

George Owen (7)
Langdale Primary School, Clayton

Slim

I'm yellow and smooth
I taste sweet
Have you guessed my question yet?
Monkeys love me
You have to peel off my skin to eat me
Are you getting close?
I am slim and I live in a fruit bowl
Do you know what I am?

Answer: A banana.

Evie Violet Elizabeth Capewell (7)
Langdale Primary School, Clayton

Four Paws

I am like a furry soft ball
I've got big ears
I wag my tail
I have puppies
Have you guessed me yet?
I am black and white
I'm a lovely pet.
What am I?

Answer: A dog.

Orla Hindhaugh (6)
Langdale Primary School, Clayton

Sizzle

I taste nice with ketchup
I'm brown when I'm hot
You cook me to eat me
You find me in a shop
I am popular
I smell like bacon.
What am I?

Answer: A sausage.

Edward Pointon (7)
Langdale Primary School, Clayton

Fun

When you turn me on, I am white
When you tap me, something happens
I am fun to play on
Can you guess me yet?
I can change colour.
What am I?

Answer: A whiteboard.

Ava Nadin (7)
Langdale Primary School, Clayton

Big Farm

I have a ring through my nose
I am scared of red
I am like a cow
I am black
I have a tail
I have horns
I can hurt you.
What am I?

Answer: A bull.

Kian Morgan (6)
Langdale Primary School, Clayton

Grey Scary Beast

I have a long trunk
I have big ears
I have a swishy tail
I am big and grey
Do you know what I am yet?
I drink water.
What am I?

Answer: An elephant.

Vivienne Burke (6)
Langdale Primary School, Clayton

Muddy

I've got a curly tail
I have pointy floppy ears
Have you guessed me yet?
I am pink
I grunt
I love mud.
What am I?

Answer: A pig.

Charlotte Brunt (7)
Langdale Primary School, Clayton

Nut Eater

I have a big bushy tail
I can be red or brown
I eat nuts
Have you guessed me yet?
I am a good jumper.
What am I?

Answer: A squirrel.

Franklin Garvey (7)
Langdale Primary School, Clayton

Nut Eater

I eat nuts
I am brown
You see me up in trees
Have you guessed me yet?
I'm little.
What am I?

Answer: A squirrel.

Charlotte Lello (7)
Langdale Primary School, Clayton

Superhero

I have a mask
I defeat the Joker
I hate the Dark Knight
I have a green mask.
Who am I?

Answer: Robin.

Hudhaifa AlGhannam (7)
Langdale Primary School, Clayton

Bang And Crash

I light up the sky
I go up really high
Make sure you stand
I could whack
I do loads of crackling
I am really loud
I am colourful, I bang and crash
I am sometimes big and sometimes small
People think I'm beautiful.
What am I?

Answer: A firework.

Florence Smith (7)
Moorgate Primary Academy, Moorgate

A Rainforest Riddle

I have silky, golden and gleaming speckled fur
My coat is soft with black spots
I crouch and I pounce
Suddenly I see a juicy monkey
I grab the juicy monkey and I gobble it up.
What am I?

Answer: A leopard.

Myla McKay-Hunter (5)
Moorgate Primary Academy, Moorgate

The Predator

I have sharp scary claws
I have a long tail
I am scary because I eat prey
I have black stripes
I have smooth fur
I have sharp teeth
I live in the wild jungle.
What am I?

Answer: A tiger.

Jasmine Krumina (6)
Moorgate Primary Academy, Moorgate

Little Riddlers 2018 - Staffordshire

Teeth In The Pool

I live in the sea
I have a pointy fin
I eat fish
I am not your friend
I have blue skin
I have sharp teeth
I could kill anybody
I am very big and scary.
What am I?

Answer: A shark.

Blake Antony McNeill (6)
Moorgate Primary Academy, Moorgate

A Rainforest Riddle

I have vibrant and colourful skin
My coat is slimy and sticky
I bounce when I see food
Suddenly I see a juicy bug
I dart my tongue out and gobble it up.
What am I?

Answer: A poison dart frog.

Bethany Hunt (5)
Moorgate Primary Academy, Moorgate

Little Riddlers 2018 - Staffordshire

The Slithering Creature

I am a reptile
I can be different patterns and colours
I can slither
I have a long tongue
I have a long body
You can keep me as a pet
I like mice.
What am I?

Answer: A snake.

Corey Dempster (6)
Moorgate Primary Academy, Moorgate

In The Shady Forest

I am a hairy mammal
I live in a shady rainy forest
I swing from tree to tree
I have a long tail
I eat fruit that is yellow
I am very cheeky.
What am I?

Answer: A monkey.

Le-Ha Dao (7)
Moorgate Primary Academy, Moorgate

King Of The Water

I have white sharp teeth
I have four short legs
I wade in the water
Suddenly I see a bird for my tea
Gobble, gobble, gobble, it's gone!
What am I?

Answer: A crocodile.

Jayden Ollie Ryley (5)
Moorgate Primary Academy, Moorgate

A Rainforest Riddle

I have a smooth coat
My coat is cuddly and silky
I clamber across the mossy trees
Suddenly I see a juicy banana
I grab the juicy banana.
What am I?

Answer: A monkey.

Maja Joanna Rynkun (5)
Moorgate Primary Academy, Moorgate

In The Lake

I jump a lot
I like eating fleas
I am very green and slimy
I am not a mammal
Some of my kind are poisonous
I lie on a lily pad.
What am I?

Answer: A frog.

Molly Olivia Seal (7)
Moorgate Primary Academy, Moorgate

I Am At The Vets

I have four legs
I like to lick water
I eat fish
I am furry
I live on some people's houses
I am small
I hate dogs.
What am I?

Answer: A cat.

Daisy Kathleen Brookes (7)
Moorgate Primary Academy, Moorgate

A Little Pet

I have four paws
I have a tail
I eat meat
I chew teddies
I drink water
I don't like cats
I go *woof-woof*.
What am I?

Answer: A dog.

James Ian John Thompson (7)
Moorgate Primary Academy, Moorgate

Slithering Through The Jungle

I have a long tail
I have lots of scales
I slither across the floor
Suddenly I see a mouse for my tea.
Munch, munch, munch.
What am I?

Answer: A snake.

Peyton Mills-Deakin (5)
Moorgate Primary Academy, Moorgate

A Rainforest Riddle

My coat is grey and white
I swing across the dark canopy
Suddenly I see a juicy berry
I clamber to it and gobble it up.
What am I?

Answer: A sloth.

Lacey-Rae Reynolds (6)
Moorgate Primary Academy, Moorgate

Down On The Ground

I am small
I live in the Amazon
I'm an arachnid
I have six eyes
I can be a pet.
I have eight legs.
What am I?

Answer: A tarantula.

Seb Hunt (6)
Moorgate Primary Academy, Moorgate

The Long Neck

I have sticky-up ears
I like to eat hay
I am dotty
I am furry
I have long eyelashes
I have a long neck.
What am I?

Answer: A giraffe.

Shayla Ann Crowley (6)
Moorgate Primary Academy, Moorgate

The Fearsome Animal

I like to play ball
I like going for a walk
I have sharp claws
I can run fast
I am furry
I wag my tail.
What am I?

Answer: A dog.

Jayden Marsh (6)
Moorgate Primary Academy, Moorgate

In The Grass

I eat meat
I have soft fur
I have four legs
I have sharp teeth
I have a fluffy tail
I have a big mane.
What am I?

Answer: A lion.

Mason Yeo Powles (7)
Moorgate Primary Academy, Moorgate

Spot Me If You Can

I have four medium-sized legs
I have silky golden fur
I can run at speed
Suddenly I see a zebra for my tea.
What am I?

Answer: A leopard.

Oscar Friend (5)
Moorgate Primary Academy, Moorgate

Up In A Tree

I have wings
I have fluffy feathers
I eat worms
I do not flutter
I have two legs
I sometimes walk.
What am I?

Answer: A bird.

Maggie Pemperton (6)
Moorgate Primary Academy, Moorgate

The Mysterious Library

People can read me
I have no legs
It is hard to find me
I tell stories
I have pages
I have letters.
What am I?

Answer: A book.

Ethan Andrew Bennett (7)
Moorgate Primary Academy, Moorgate

The Fast Creature

I have a small head
I have spots
I have four legs
I live in Africa
I catch animals
I run fast.
What am I?

Answer: A cheetah.

Alfie Patrick Butler (5)
Moorgate Primary Academy, Moorgate

The Whizzing Runner

I have spots
I run really fast
I climb trees
I have pointy knees
I live in Africa
I am yellow.
What am I?

Answer: A cheetah.

Erin Rose James (6)
Moorgate Primary Academy, Moorgate

A Fluffy Ball

I have four legs
I have soft fur
I don't bark
I like milk
I don't like dogs
I eat fish.
What am I?

Answer: A cat.

Arnav Singh (6)
Moorgate Primary Academy, Moorgate

The Predator

I have orange and black stripes
I like to roar
I eat meat
I live in the jungle
I hide behind trees.
What am I?

Answer: A tiger.

Bethany-Rose Silver (6)
Moorgate Primary Academy, Moorgate

In The Garden

I have a soft body
I have four legs
I like fish
I like mice
I live in a house
I have four paws.
What am I?

Answer: A cat.

Dante McGrath (7)
Moorgate Primary Academy, Moorgate

A Rainforest Riddle

I have a coat that is gold,
I have gleaming eyes,
I creep and I prowl,
I like to eat a tasty monkey.
What am I?

Answer: A leopard.

Albie George Hollis (5)
Moorgate Primary Academy, Moorgate

Little Riddlers 2018 - Staffordshire

King Of The Water

I am a super fast swimmer
I have pointy fins
I have sharp teeth
I eat other fish
I like to bite.
What am I?

Answer: A shark.

Luca Bishop (5)
Moorgate Primary Academy, Moorgate

The Fast Swimmer

I live in water
I am different colours
I swim fast
I have fins, not feet
I have a swishing tail.
What am I?

Answer: A fish.

Emanuela Ayline Bogdan (6)
Moorgate Primary Academy, Moorgate

Little Riddlers 2018 - Staffordshire

The Roller

I roll in mud
I have a curly tail
I am pink
I eat flies
I have little eyes
I live on a farm
What am I?

Answer: A pig.

Lucy Hughes (6)
Moorgate Primary Academy, Moorgate

A Munching Monster

I have four legs
I love running
I like munching bones
I don't like cats
I have sharp teeth.
What am I?

Answer: A dog.

Alina Mihaela Lungu (7)
Moorgate Primary Academy, Moorgate

King Of The Water

I have sharp spikes
I have sharp teeth
I am a monster
I am as green as can be
I eat meat.
What am I?

Answer: A crocodile.

Jayden Jennings (6)
Moorgate Primary Academy, Moorgate

Slithering Through The Jungle

I am full of colourful patterns
I have beady eyes
I go slither, slither
I do not have any legs.
What am I?

Answer: A snake.

Lola Holly Brennan (5)
Moorgate Primary Academy, Moorgate

The Small-Clawed Animal

I have sharp claws
I am small
I have stripes
I like mice
I am soft
I have orange eyes.
What am I?

Answer: A cat.

Henry Hinkley (6)
Moorgate Primary Academy, Moorgate

The Bone Eater

I run fast
I am so cute
I have brown eyes
I have brown fur
I can bark
I wag my tail.
What am I?

Answer: A dog.

Oscar Harvey Duerden (6)
Moorgate Primary Academy, Moorgate

A Rainforest Riddle

I have a soft silky coat
I have muddy feet
I climb up a tree
I see a juicy monkey.
What am I?

Answer: A leopard.

Lilly Bonkowska (5)
Moorgate Primary Academy, Moorgate

Spotty

I have four legs
I have black spots
I run fast
Suddenly I see a zebra for my tea.
What am I?

Answer: A leopard.

Christian-Denis Ionita (5)
Moorgate Primary Academy, Moorgate

Little Riddlers 2018 - Staffordshire

Slither, Slither, Quick, Quick

I have no legs
I have orange scales and I slither
Suddenly I see a mouse for my tea.
What am I?

Answer: A snake.

Isla Louise De,aubeney James (5)
Moorgate Primary Academy, Moorgate

The Fast Runner

I am fast
I am spotty
I am yellow
I live in Africa
I eat meat.
What am I?

Answer: A cheetah.

Emilia Jurkiewicz (6)
Moorgate Primary Academy, Moorgate

The Beautiful One

My body is long but not as long as a dragonfly's body
My wings are beautiful
My friends have different coloured wings
I start out being a caterpillar
My colours are so beautiful
I eat the nectar from flowers
I fly from flower to flower but
I am not a bee.
What am I?

Answer: A butterfly.

Melody Sentulio (6)
St Augustine's RC (A) Primary School, Meir

A Flying Bug

I have two sets of wings
I eat small bugs
I can be found on a leaf
I can fly around your house
I can climb walls
I cannot be found easily
I have black spots and I am red.
What am I?

Answer: A ladybird.

Alphonsina Nsimi (6)
St Augustine's RC (A) Primary School, Meir

Black

My body is strong
I have three parts to my body
I have six legs
I have two antennae
My antennae are black
I can walk while I am pushing my food around
I am black.
What am I?

Answer: A beetle.

George Ikins (5)
St Augustine's RC (A) Primary School, Meir

The Crawler Black Bug

I am black and I can crawl
I have three parts to my back
I have black clicking legs
Some of my kind can be red like fire
I am so small you might not see me
I am strong.
What am I?

Answer: An ant.

Lydia Freyah Minister (6)
St Augustine's RC (A) Primary School, Meir

Flyer

I can fly to other countries
I can eat nectar or leaves
I can have a baby
I can fly to flowers
I can change my colours
I have black eggs.
What am I?

Answer: A butterfly.

Oliver Grajcar (6)
St Augustine's RC (A) Primary School, Meir

Flying Free

I fly through the air and
I sit on the ground
I eat nectar
I have antennae
I have lovely patterns
I fly to homes
I am so colourful.
What am I?

Answer: A butterfly.

Hibbah Amin (5)
St Augustine's RC (A) Primary School, Meir

Spotty Flyer

I have three body parts
I am an insect
I sleep on a leaf
I fly above the ground
I prefer flying than watching
I have black spots.
What am I?

Answer: A ladybird.

Jenson Bayley Ayres (6)
St Augustine's RC (A) Primary School, Meir

Flying Spots

I have wings that can fly in the sky
I have spots on my wings
I have six legs
I have antennae
I am red and black.
What am I?

Answer: A ladybird.

Tiffany Maziwisa (6)
St Augustine's RC (A) Primary School, Meir

Flying Bugs

I have two parts to my body
My antennae are big
I can fly anywhere
I look different when I am little.
What am I?

Answer: A butterfly.

Indie Anna Mary Reynolds (6)
St Augustine's RC (A) Primary School, Meir

The Green Bug

I have green legs
I live on grass
I am alive in the sun
I am alive on the plants
I hop.
What am I?

Answer: A grasshopper.

Tayden Arif Gratton (5)
St Augustine's RC (A) Primary School, Meir

Flying High

I love watching the sky, I'm a beautiful object flying high
I always travel on a holiday
I take people to where they want to go.
What am I?

Answer: An aeroplane.

Arahbela Arvesu (6)
St John's CE (A) Primary School, Trent Vale

The Smelly Gang

I am smelly
I can be short
I can be long
You can wear me
You can wash me
I can be spotty
I can be stripy
I can be any colour
I can be any size
I can't move
I can be pretty
I can be ugly.
What am I?

Answer: A sock.

Scarlett Pearson (5)
St Peter's CE First School, Marchington

Little Riddlers 2018 - Staffordshire

The Yummy Piece

Lots of people eat me
People can eat me in any month
I am not a person and not an animal
You would like to eat me on sunny days
You also eat me on special days
You can put candles on me.
What am I?

Answer: A cake.

Joseph Orme (6)
St Peter's CE First School, Marchington

What Am I?

I work for the Queen
I am tough
I wear a big bearskin hat
I have medals
You see me outside the Queen's palace
I wear a red jacket with gold and black.
What am I?

Answer: A guardsman.

William Stanley Goodwin (6)
St Peter's CE First School, Marchington

Mr Eager

I am long
I have a big nose
I hide from people
I always go fast
I can cut wood
I am brown
I live in a lake
My name starts with 'B'.
What am I?

Answer: A beaver.

Mason Joseph (7)
St Peter's CE First School, Marchington

The Barker

I have a cute smile
I have black fur
I like playing outside
I love food
I like having walks
I like chasing cats.
What am I?

Answer: A dog.

Lily Rose Hawkins (6)
St Peter's CE First School, Marchington

The Fashion

I am beautiful
I am fancy
I am black, my favourite colour
I can be worn
I have a chain to unlock
I am pretty
What am I?

Answer: A choker.

Evelyn Ball (6)
St Peter's CE First School, Marchington

The Jaws

I am long
I am fast
I'm as fast as a boat
I have sharp teeth
I have my tail in the water
I eat meat.
What am I?

Answer: A shark.

Barney Ward (6)
St Peter's CE First School, Marchington

Little Riddlers 2018 - Staffordshire

I Am As Stinky As A...

I am stinky
You can wear me
I can stretch
I can have holes
I am lots of different colours
I cannot talk.
What am I?

Answer: A sock.

Matthew Neale (6)
St Peter's CE First School, Marchington

The Red Family

I am big and round
I have a long stalk
I am shiny and have seeds inside
I am sometimes green
I cannot move.
What am I?

Answer: An apple.

Ellie Louise Buxton (7)
St Peter's CE First School, Marchington

Little Riddlers 2018 - Staffordshire

I Am As Fast As A...

I am fast
I am spotty all over
I have a long tail
I have four legs
I am orange
I'm like a lion.
What am I?

Answer: A cheetah.

Edan Hall (6)
St Peter's CE First School, Marchington

Yummy Like Them

I have seeds
I am red
I am sweet
I am yummy
You can eat me.
What am I?

Answer: A strawberry.

Sienna-Rose Horton (6)
St Peter's CE First School, Marchington

Strong Walls

I am made out of stone
You cannot break into me
I have turrets.
What am I?

Answer: A castle.

William Hayhurst (6)
St Peter's CE First School, Marchington

Silly Pants

You can wear me
I have holes
I am warm
Boys wear me
What am I?

Answer: Pants.

Korey Gildart (5)
St Peter's CE First School, Marchington

YoungWriters
Est.1991

YOUNG WRITERS INFORMATION

We hope you have enjoyed reading this book – and that you will continue to in the coming years.

If you're a young writer who enjoys reading and creative writing, or the parent of an enthusiastic poet or story writer, do visit our website www.youngwriters.co.uk. Here you will find free competitions, workshops and games, as well as recommended reads, a poetry glossary and our blog.

If you would like to order further copies of this book, or any of our other titles, then please give us a call or visit www.youngwriters.co.uk.

Young Writers
Remus House
Coltsfoot Drive
Peterborough
PE2 9BF
(01733) 890066
info@youngwriters.co.uk